Bones in the Shallows

poems from Mission Creek

BONES IN THE SHALLOWS

poems from Mission Creek

Tito Titus

for Kate

a most extraordinary pony hunter

Contents

*It's not any better here—here, there now, tomorrow, next
Wednesday—geologically speaking it's all the same millisecond.
The gentle rustle of armies crawling the planet like ants.
Anybody with any sense knows what's coming.*

—Vanessa Veselka, *The Fort of Young Saplings*

A word

We wear the weather. It wraps around us, presses upon our skin. Temperature, humidity, barometric pressure, wind speed—these elements comprise our pervasive experience of reality. To describe the weather is to describe what it feels like to be alive and sentient.

On the Beach by Nevil Shute, a best seller in its time, deeply affected me. In that novel, nuclear holocaust destroyed human life and civilization around the globe—except in Australia. Australians did their best to live normal lives while knowing they could not escape the inevitable nuclear death clouds swirling about the planet. Anxiously, they waited for the next thing—the likely last thing—to happen.

At the coffee shop on Cottage Street a few years ago, folks wondered whether climate change was real. Some clung to the hoax hypothesis; others supposed ocean currents simply brought us another *El Niño*. But now we know. We're living in our own Nevil Shute novel.

Cashmere, Washington
A valley of apples and pears

Enrique's forty acres of Walla Wallas

The sweet and sour smell—
      onions, my favorites,
      Walla Walla Sweets—

they roast before rotting
      in hot July dirt and sun
      for too many weeks.

Onions sweat in 120 degrees,
      water beads on their bulbs,
        evaporates. Leaves shrivel.

Pale blisters bake
      in record heat beneath papery skins
      wrapped beneath mushy white meat.

Enrique plows 'em under,
      again and again 'til
      soil and dead onions merge.

The seed pods, too; they died,
      killed next year's crop,
      kicked hope in the butt.

Crop insurance—too high to buy—
      won't compense this mess,
      leaves losses to eat next spring,

when Walla Walla heats.

The doggest days of August

> *It's not true that living is easy—for no creature on earth*
> *is the living easy, not even in summertime. . .*
> "I Don't Want to Spend the Rest of My Days
> Grieving" Margaret Renkl, *New York Times*,
> August 9, 2021.

The woman from Nashville,
quotes Wordsworth,
marvels at the seasonal brevity
of splendor in the grass,

says our Oregon wildfire
smoke finds its way into
the nostrils of Kentucky folks
sitting on front porches

by the road that follows the holler
down to Fraser Creek, Eagle Creek,
or Bledsoe coal mines, hellish holes
of bituminous to burn.

We trade sky-bound black billows
for the electric energy of gods,
pretend we don't know
that this is how it goes,

when summer temperatures rise
and we beat the heat by burning
coal to run air conditioners
in nursing homes and hospitals

crowded with sweaty humans
pondering how many people
it takes to make a pandemic,
or drive animals to extinction.

Mission Creek homecoming

Craggy mountains, ruthless green,
snow-shined walls,
keep coastal clouds
from creeping over our valley.

Bunched billions of apple blossoms
usher the highway headed here.
They wave, sparkle white,
smile, and say—

Welcome home, it's April!
Your lawn went crazy
while you were away,
steelhead filled your creek,
and the sunshine barely remembers
you and your squinty smile.

Alice next door, yesterday morning

Just watered my dead plants.
They bent to the ground,
brown and brittle, bowing
like conquered warriors.

Lived here all m' life, y'know,
never seen the creek so low.
You can cross it without
gettin' yer ankles wet.
Brush on the creek-bank
looks like rooted kindling,
ready to burn 'til next Sunday
and back, burn us out, y'know?

Really, Darlin', what's next?

Hydromechanics

A twig, matchstick-sized, flips
into slow water, circles
gentle eddies, twirls 'round rocks,
navigates its way
to the river—then points west.
Skeeters race to the tiny stem,
attack, then skate back, losing it.
Water's own gravity pulls hard.

I knew a man named Creek,
a stream hydraulics engineer.
He taught me channel banks
erode and accrete, depending
on water volume, speed, and direction.
Building a barrier along a bank
shoots Adam's ale to the other shore,
where it chomps dirt and rock,
eats its way across pastures,
heads toward Spokane, points east.

Twigs must love this dance.

Water and gravity

Forest fires upstream laid the ground bare,
turned mountain ravines into rain funnels,
raised a rush of water through the canyon,
tore at creek banks like an army
of front-loaders, stacked woody debris
at the bridges, flooded the roads.

So-called smart people protected their own—
built concrete bulkheads and rip-rap walls
along the banks, turned the creek
into a concrete ditch, a chute to the sea,
that washed away spawning beds,
dirtied the river below.

Life is like that it seems—
problems come from upstream.

Wilfred, if you ask him

Them environmental folks,
      they got no sense.

They want fences
      to follow stream-sides
      fifty feet back from both banks.

Let it be natural, they say—
      brush, vines, poison oak,
      blackberries, no doubt.

Protect the fish, they claim—
Protect the fish!? Hah—
      as if the damn creek
      had fish anymore!

I got a hundred head of cattle
      need a place to drink
      and shit.

The environmentals, they don't
      understand economics,
      how people need beef.

I paid big money for this land;
      they want to take it,
      not pay a penny.

It's a damn fifty-foot-wide land grab.
      It's my property, f 'chrissake—
      not theirs to take!

Last year's dry spell

Sizzling hot rocks radiate the day
where the river used to be.

> *I didn't mean for it*
> *to be this way.*

Tall amber grass—creekbank fire fuel—
doesn't wave. No wind.

> *I don't know what I thought,*
> *if I thought at all..*

Twenty-four homes in the city
burned to the ground.

> *Regret—*
> *too fancy a word.*

Big hot numbers with torrid stories,
shroud our wilted landscape.

> *Disappearance looks like:*
> *this.*

Dead salmon don't spawn.
Eaten by beetles, trees rush to blaze.

> *I am so sorry.*

This year's dry spell

Never saw the creek so low.

It's a hot night.

Dust clutches powdery brown grass.

Yeah, triple-digit temps.

My prayer flags hang dead in still air.

Thayze no breeze, Mama!

Smoke turns the scimitar moon orange.

A science fiction sky.

You could hear the creek last night, its burble.

But can you hear it now?

Apocalypse on Mission Creek

> *I sat in the dark and thought: There's no big apocalypse.*
> *Just an endless procession of little ones.*
> —Neil Gaiman, *Signal to Noise*

It's gone!
The fucker's gone!
Damn creek dried up.

Dry rocks, umber mud,
barely damp in the shade—
cottonwood, maple, elm, fir, pine.

Cricket songs seem sad,
now wails not chirps—
a terrible mourning.

The fish, they left us
weeks ago, gills filled
with warm water fungi.

What's a pond turtle to do?
It's sad to end a poem
with an ugly word, but here we are:

Extirpation.

**Take a little walk with me, Arlene,
and tell me, What do you love?**

From bridge to bridge, I walked
the dead creek bed, stumbling
over hot rocks and dark damp silt,
found three granola bar wrappers,
blue, white, and red foil for the folks,
three plastic water bottles, capped,
discovered Pepsi's popularity
(eight cans to Coke's one),
a white vinyl chair,
black plastic sacks, now hueless and hoary,
two muddy silver-and-blue Bud Light cans,
a green Monster liquid energy bottle,
a hair net, a medical face mask,
three shiny blue Doritos bags
(one, half-full of toxic orange chips),
twelve salmon, pink flesh rotting
in the swelter of day,
white bones breaking through—
too young to spawn,
too dead to know.

In a blackwater puddle
minnows and fingerlings
make a quiet commotion,
chase around in tree shadows.

Life longs for itself.

The water's side-job

Like a drunk too late for dinner,
the creek straggled back this evening,
slowly slipped into its bed, murmuring,
I was upstream, Hon—watering orchards.
They took me at their will,
raped me like English Lords.

Thus, it's decreed:
Better you eat pears than fish.

21st Century ethics

Like a kid in a candy store
or a staggering drunk in a shooting gallery,

like an oil man in Araby
or an addict in the alley,

like a priest faltering in faith
or a farmer who wants more water,

we make our way, make our choices—
we succumb to our sins.

October coming down

How do you describe a creek?
Twenty cubic feet per second, the engineer said.

I toss a slender woody shoot,
watch it meander through ripples,
fouette through eddies,
dive from glittering rocks,
float toward the Wenatchee River—
a one-legged ballerina, dancing
toward the ravenous Columbia.
Past the equinox now, the creek
runs ten-feet wide, a few inches deep.

Still, no rain.

Now I know—in this parched tenth month—
how much water the upstream orchards
swallowed when fish rotted on dry rocks:
enough to seduce innocent Coho
climbing freshwater reaches,
unaware of the Mission Creek murders
of their cousins, only a month before.

Twenty cubic feet per second,
enough to pretend the drought is done.

Dry cycle

Who by fire?

—Leonard Cohen

The grass, amazing green leaves, how fast they grabbed the early spring hillsides, only a winter after the fire that scrambled over those hills like hell-in-a-hurry, then burst into town like a thousand acre flaming tsunami, leaped over rooftops, scorched businesses, burned twenty-four homes, and torched warehouses to the ground with its wind-borne sparks.

So lovely, hillside green shadows undulating in spring; but summer comes again, grass fades early, blades turn brown and brittle, ready to burn when a white-hot shot of lightening cracks open the sky and electric energy sparks parched air, ignites feverish fuel, tosses flaming tumbleweeds across highways and once verdant fields.

The Okanagan-Wenatchee National Fire

It was a hell storm up here.
—Okanogan County Sheriff
Frank Rogers, *CNN*

Our summer highway landscape
smells like a dirty fireplace,
fried tractor tires, smoking cow hides.

It spreads charred-black mile upon mile,
barns, fences, sheds, and doublewides.
where lightning struck the fatwood.

Trees, grass, brush—dried by drought,
brown needles and leaves,
split grey fence posts, and paintless

pens and sheds, once rust-brown
by countless summer suns, now
sooty shadows of cattlemen's dreams.

Across the Inland Empire—Upper Falls,
Carlton, Carpenter Road, Tunk Block,
Coluckum Tarps, Wolverine, Stickpin,

Cougar Creek, Highway 8, Sleepy Hollow,
Saddle Lakes, Twisp River, Graves Mountain,
where ranches and livestock used to be.

Innocents—deer, elk, and bear;
helpless—goats, llamas, chickens;
trapped—three men, ages 31, 26, and 20.

Gaia knows where you live

> *What mankind must know is that human beings*
> *cannot live without Mother Earth, but*
> *the planet can live without humans.*
> —Evo Morales, President of
> Bolivia, 2006 to 2019

She has ice worms and roaches,
desert rats, phytoplankton,
spiders, survivors of ancient infernos.
Microbes swim in her freezing sky
thirty-thousand feet above her oceans.
She feeds things that live in the dark.

When your fumbling stokes her air,
heats it up, bakes it, she becomes touchwood,
blazes like an angry beast
chasing summer winds.
When you burn her, she will smoke you.

When we cut her open, she bleeds
in her streams and rivers, freshly noxious.
Sandworms and slime will survive;
life will continue, with or without us.
Not to worry, she'll do fine when we're gone.

Here comes the sun

It's April again. The Creek roars white,
gets fat in the middle, runs waves
like a river, sucks mountain snowmelt
with days that warm too soon.

I hang grape and kiwi vines in nooses
made from green garden twine,
stretched across new growth
beneath a toasty morning sun.

Coffee cup in hand, I listen
to the weather on my pocket radio
dangling from a splintered gray stake,
then pause, shake my head—

like yesterday and the day before
a man's airwave voice reports
another week of blue sky days
in the valley of apples and pears.

Ladies and gentlemen, the ama-a-zing heat dome!

Kindling-hot winds press my flesh.
It's a real thing; but not a *heat wave*
(something common, like a new salon do).
That's so twentieth century, Dearie!

Now we have domes! *Heat domes*!
They squat—fat, flat, and wide,
like Jabba the Hutt squatting
over thirteen western states;

Hutt butt chunks up against the Rockies,
Jabba-belly hangs over the Pacific coast.
We live in the new little shop of horrors:
with our fevered heat-dome-Jabba,

hungry to keep forests and towns ablaze,
raise the mercury above memory,
bake babies and old ladies,
kill groceries rooted in dry dirt.

Screaming trees

> *You can actually hear a tree dying.*
> —Maya Wei-Haas,
> "What Does a Dying Forest
> Sound Like?" *Smithsonian,*
> April 2016

Ultrasonic pops, faster than a human ear,
come from bubbles, cavitations—
air trapped in the xylem
somewhere between begging roots
and desiccating canopy.

As trees collect carbon dioxide
they open their pores—
but it's no beauty treatment;
it causes water loss,
so precious in late summer.

Biologists, physiologists, scientists,
pace around the tree, waiting
for its screams, its bursting balloons,
to tell a listening machine made by engineers
the story of its staggering march to death.

Thirsty wood makes its own moan:
the sound of detonating air blisters
plugging the vertical aqueducts
that watered its latter day leaves—
a secret weeping for life leaving itself.

Summer in the time of Corona

My armpits,
      they're hot pockets—
they smell like August
      in the turning-point year
when northerners bought
their first air conditioners
and my dead mother revolved
      like a roast on a rotisserie
in her shady mausoleum, saying,
just as she said when she was alive:
      I told you, I told you!
      It's getting hotter
      and I can't breathe in this air.

I like to sweat,
      feel it trickle on my ribs,
but never thought
      it'd come to this—a semicolon
in a viral pandemic sentence that says,
      You ain't seen nothin' yet;
      now arrive the climate clarions,
      trumpets ablare, come to declare—
      something incredible is about to happen.

The lazy man's guide

Beside this wooded creekside haven,
I watch the days, how they swim too fast,
too slippery for an old man to hold.

The summer sun charges toward autumn,
shouts, *today exceeds yesterday,*
but you haven't seen tomorrow!

My reservoir of morning suns—they wash
down life's drain like the mountain snowmelt
that ransacks creekbanks in its frantic rush

to the river, westbound to the Pacific.
Each morning I misplace my wisdom,
sometimes find it as the day lies down to die.

Night reminds me of what's real,
and I grieve the squandered hours,
ruminate too much.

On my deathbed, I'll say, *Ahhhhh!*
Nowwwwww I see! Then mumble
something about wanting *just one more dance.*

Last summer on Mission Creek

This is the last time I'll play here.

—Jerry Jeff Walker, Contrary to Ordinary

Sumac leaves, stark and dark green,
wrestle summer winds.

Creek burbles play. Their watery laughter
climbs our woody bank.

Sunlight snakes through the cottonwoods,
spotlights between wet shadows.

Blue sky, cloudless again today,
brightens my peppers and pears.

Power lines run the ridgelines:
sun-warmed spider silk on Athena's breast.

Flat farmlands nudge the feet of flashing
green mountains, steep as pine.

My life became more beautiful than I knew,
and faster, too!

I spent it searching for summer, yet missed it
by inches most years.

Phallic Staghorn sumac flowers grow streamside—
thick, red, and fuzzy in autumn;

they point skyward from the tips of slender limbs;
without embarrassment or regret, they shine.

Your life, civilization, and everything

Tarry not, for Time's door—
it's always closing.

The horsemen—
they're just over the border,
coming this way.

Did you forget something?
Decide now.

Reality looks like this:
unseasonably warm.

CODA

The fire next time

A shovel on my shoulder,
    I followed an oil-belching D-9 Cat.
        It's blade scraped rocky ridgelines;
        the diesel roared, steel tracks shrieked.

Wildfire raged below us, forty feet per flame,
    climbed upward, full-tilt toward
        our craggy hogback,
        while the D-9 and I

stripped away burnable life,
    eradicated sage brush and bunch grass,
        that could carry flames
        across our windy ridgetop.

Midnight flames glowed in the rock-bottom gully,
    grass-smoke danced like snakes in firelight,
        gray gossamer wraiths forewarning—
        here comes the big burn.

After a twenty-four hour shift,
    I slept beneath a two-ton truck,
        baked in its hot oily shade, thirsty, tired,
        ate cold stew from a military can,

excited, ready to go home or fight wildfire,
    whichever—it didn't matter;
        I was sixteen, making good money,
        but afraid I didn't belong.

Sixty years later, seas of flames—firestorms—
       sweep Siberia, Australia, California, Oregon,
           Alaska, British Columbia, the world,
       and this valley of orchards I live in.

My history prepared me for this,
       but I'm still not ready for the next big burn.

Notes

Thanks to Scott Ezell for your tireless and thorough editorial and
organizational review of these poems and for your
publication guidance, design, and structural contribution to
this book.

Thanks to Priscilla Long, Bethany Reid, and Ian Sanquist for
your generous developmental review and recommendations.

Thanks to Mike O'Connor—Buddhist poet, teacher, friend,
mentor, Chinese translator—for your years of kind and
thoughtful coaching.

Thanks to Andrew Murdoch, Washington State Department of
Fisheries and Wildlife research scientist, for providing
background information and for establishing a fish
monitoring facility on Mission Creek after learning the
genesis of the poem "Take a little walk with me, Arlene, and
tell me, what do you love?"

Thanks to Dionne Haroutunian whose cover illustration stole my
heart from the get-go.

The phrase *Life's longing for itself* comes from Kahlil Gibran,
The Prophet, "On Children":
 And a woman who held a babe against her bosom said,
  "Speak to us of Children."
 And he said:
 Your children are not your children.
 They are the sons and daughters of Life's longing for itself.

The title "Take a little walk with me, Arlene, and tell me, what do you love?" paraphrases Bo Diddley's lyric "Who do you love?"

The title "Screaming trees" comes from the late poet, lyricist, musician, and performing artist Mark Lanegan and his band of the same name.

"Amid last summer's drought and heat wave, some 98 percent of Okanogan basin sockeye salmon died before they reached upstream spawning grounds."
    "Last year's heat wave doomed nearly all Okanogan sockeye salmon," *The Seattle Times*, April 2016 indentation?

"Fishing for fall chinook is now banned in multiple rivers on Oregon's north coast because extremely dry conditions have fueled a widespread die-off of the species."
    "Dry conditions fuel salmon die-off on Oregon coast," *The Associated Press*, December 16, 2019.

"On the edge of a cherry orchard Thursday morning, under a smoky gray sky, Francisco Martinez and his crew milled about before starting work. For Martinez, a crew supervisor, it was a routine morning. But once he started looking at the trees he saw things he'd never seen before. Some of the Sweetheart cherries dangling from branches on the orchard's border didn't look right. They were wizened, skins wrinkled like big red raisins."
    "Shriveled and burned: Extreme temps take a toll on Washington fruit industry," *The Spokesman Review*, Spokane, July 28, 2021.

"The U.S. Forest Service on Thursday identified the three
     firefighters who were killed battling a fast-growing wildfire
     in Washington state as Tom Zbyszewski, 20, Andrew Zajac,
     26, and Richard Wheeler, 31. The men, all members of an
     engine crew from Okanogan-Wenatchee National Forest in
     central Washington, died Wednesday after their vehicle
     crashed and was overtaken by flames near the town of
     Twisp. The fire spread quickly and erratically, driven by
     wind and feeding on drought-parched land, the agency
     said."
                    "Three Firefighters Killed in Washington Blaze
                         Identified," Alex Johnson, *NBC News,* Aug. 21,
                         2015. Indentation?

"The heat wave baking the U.S. Pacific Northwest and British
     Columbia, Canada, is of an intensity never recorded by
     modern humans. By one measure it is more rare than a once
     in a 1,000 year event. . . This heat wave comes on the heels
     of another historic heat wave less than two weeks ago that
     baked the U.S. Intermountain West, Desert Southwest and
     California with hundreds of record highs."
                    Jeff Berardelli, "Pacific Northwest bakes under once-
                         in-a-millennium heat dome," *CBS News,* June 29,
                         2021.

"Heat waves now occur three times as often as they did in the
     1960s — on average at least six times a year in the United
     States in the 2010s. Record-breaking hot months are
     occurring five times more often than would be expected
     without global warming. And heat waves have become
     larger, affecting 25 percent more land area in the Northern
     Hemisphere than they did in 1980; including ocean areas,
     heat waves grew 50 percent."

"That Heat Dome? Yeah, It's Climate Change,"
Michael E. Mann, professor of atmospheric
science, director of the Earth System Science
Center, Pennsylvania State University, *The New
York Times*, June 29, 2021.

"The fire next time" was originally published as "When I was a
fireman," *The Prairie Lights Review*, Vol. 44, No. 1, 2021.
Available at: https://dc.cod.edu/plr/vol44/iss1/74

Thanks to Kate Titus, my beloved partner and playmate. Without
your loving support, I'd only be spitting in the wind.

Author

Tito Titus is the author of the poetry collection *I can still smile like Errol Flynn* (Empty Bowl Press, 2015). In 2020 he appeared on Garrison Keillor's "The Writer's Almanac," and in 2023, he contributed to *I Sing the Salmon Home*, an anthology curated by former Washington State Poet Laureate Rena Priest. Tito's satire appeared in *Puget Soundings*, *Argus*, and the *Seattle Post-Intelligencer*, and his poetry has appeared in various journals and anthologies.

Originally from Snake River's Hells Canyon, North America's deepest gorge, Tito worked on farms and ranches, fought range fires, barked in a carnival, went to war overseas, earned a master's in urban planning, ran for public office, joined a theater troupe, and created art. He worked as an environmental public hearings officer for eighteen years, served two terms on the Seattle Design Commission, and received the 2003 Martin Luther King Humanitarian Award from King County, Washington, for his service to elderly homeless people. Now in their eighties, Tito and his wife Kate live in Seattle and have been married forty years.